BUDGET JUSTIFICATIONS

The United States
Department of the Interior

and Performance Information
Fiscal Year 2014

NATIONAL INDIAN GAMING COMMISSION

DEPARTMENT OF THE INTERIOR
NATIONAL INDIAN GAMING COMMISSION

Fiscal Year 2014 Budget Justification

Table of Contents

Tab:Executive Summary

National Indian Gaming Commission (NIGC)

Executive Summary

The National Indian Gaming Commission (NIGC or "Commission") was created by the Indian Gaming Regulatory Act of 1988 (P.L. 100-497). The Indian Gaming Regulatory Act (IGRA) created a mechanism whereby NIGC operations are funded by the fees collected from tribal gaming operations. When the Commission began operations in February 1992, the Indian gaming industry generated revenue of about $3 billion per year. The Commission itself operated on a budget of $2.2 million with 33 full-time employees and with oversight responsibilities for approximately 200 gaming operations. As with many emerging industries, Indian gaming experienced consistent growth. Today, there are over 400 Indian gaming operations in 28 states. Revenues over the past few years suggest that the industry has stabilized with the moderate growth largely attributable to the expansion of existing facilities and the opening of new facilities on existing Indian lands.

The governmental entities regulating Indian gaming have grown along with the industry. In addition to the Commission, there are approximately 200 Tribal Gaming Commissions serving as the primary regulators of Indian gaming. Further, each of the 28 Indian gaming states provides regulatory support to implement their respective responsibilities under IGRA and tribal-state compacts. In addition to NIGC, tribal and state regulatory agencies, the Department of the Interior, the Department of Justice, the Federal Bureau of Investigation, the Internal Revenue Service, and the Department of the Treasury all implement and enforce laws that serve to ensure that tribes are the primary beneficiaries of Indian gaming. The NIGC coordinates closely with all of these governmental entities to fulfill Congress' mandates in IGRA.

In May 2006, Congress enacted the Native American Technical Corrections Act of 2006 (P.L. 109-22). This Act authorizes the Commission to collect up to 0.080 percent of the gross gaming revenue but it also links NIGC's fee collections to the growth, or contraction, of the Indian gaming industry so that the agency's funding reflects the financial status of the industry. Secondarily, the Act identified training and technical assistance as an agency function.

The fiscal year 2014 budget will continue to focus on improving governmental coordination and expanding tribal consultation, providing training and technical assistance to tribal gaming commissions and operations, conducting a regulatory review, examining and assessing the efficiency and effectiveness of the Commission, and enhancing the information technology infrastructure.

Mission

To work within the framework created by the Indian Gaming Regulatory Act (IGRA) for the regulation of gaming activities conducted by sovereign Indian tribes on Indian lands to fully realize IGRA's goals: (1) promoting tribal economic development, self-sufficiency and strong tribal governments; (2) maintaining the integrity of the Indian gaming industry; and (3) ensuring that tribes are the primary beneficiaries of their gaming activities.

Vision

The Commission's vision is to adhere to the principles of good government, including transparency and agency accountability; to promote fiscal responsibility; to operate with consistency and clarity to ensure fairness in the administration of IGRA; and to respect the capabilities and responsibilities of each sovereign Indian tribe in order to fully promote tribal economic development, self-sufficiency and strong tribal governments.

General Statement

The Indian Gaming Regulatory Act established, within the Department of the Interior, the National Indian Gaming Commission, and provided it with independent Federal regulatory authority. IGRA was enacted to support and promote tribal economic development, self-sufficiency and strong tribal governments through the operation of gaming on Indian lands. The Act provides a regulatory framework to shield Indian gaming from corruption, and to ensure that the games offered are fair and honest and that tribes are the primary beneficiaries of gaming operations. The Act created the Commission to protect tribal gaming as a means of generating revenue for tribal communities.

The Commission monitors tribal gaming activity, inspects gaming premises, conducts background investigations and audits of Class II gaming operations (and Class III gaming operations, upon request or as provided by applicable law, such as tribal gaming ordinances and tribal-state compacts). The Commission also provides technical assistance and training to tribal gaming commissions and operations and, when appropriate, undertakes enforcement actions.

The Commission fulfills its responsibilities under IGRA by:

- regulating and monitoring certain aspects of Indian gaming;
- coordinating its regulatory responsibilities with tribal regulatory agencies through

the review and approval of tribal gaming ordinances and management agreements;

- reviewing the backgrounds of individuals and entities to ensure the suitability of those seeking to engage or invest in Indian gaming;

- overseeing and reviewing the conduct and regulation of Indian gaming operations;

- referring law enforcement matters to appropriate Tribal, Federal and State entities; and

- when necessary, undertaking enforcement actions for violations of IGRA, NIGC's regulations and tribal gaming ordinances, including imposing appropriate sanctions for such violations.

As the Commission fulfills these responsibilities, it pays close attention to any indications of corrupting influences, such as those posed by organized crime and persons known to be attracted to cash-intensive industries, such as gaming.

IGRA authorizes the Commission to assess and collect fees on tribal gaming revenues to cover agency operating costs. The NIGC also conducts background investigations, including fingerprinting, of individuals and entities with a financial interest in, or management responsibility for, potential management contracts. These investigations are conducted to determine whether the management contracts can be approved. The Commission is reimbursed periodically by the potential contractors for performing these investigative services. The Commission is also reimbursed for fingerprint processing costs.

The Commission, as an agency of the Federal government, maintains a trust relationship with Indian nations. Consistent with Executive Order 13175, signed by President Clinton on November 6, 2000, the Commission is committed to meaningful consultation with tribes prior to making changes to regulations or policies having tribal implications. Additionally, the Commission endeavors to provide tribes with courteous and timely responses to issues as they arise. In all phases of its regulatory performance, the Commission and its staff observe the due process rights of those who come before it. The Commission strives to be responsive to tribes seeking guidance as they enter the Indian gaming industry, monitors trends in tribal government gaming, and reports its findings to Congress and the Administration.

The Indian Gaming Regulatory Act (IGRA) of 1988

In 1987, the Supreme Court affirmed the sovereign authority of tribes to operate and regulate gaming facilities on Indian lands free from state regulation if the state did not prohibit gaming. *California v. Cabazon Band of Indians*, 480 U.S. 202, 1987. The following year, Congress enacted the Indian Gaming Regulatory Act. Embodied in IGRA was a compromise between state and tribal interests. The drafters "balance[d] the need for sound enforcement of gaming laws and regulations, with a strong Federal interest in preserving the sovereign rights of tribal governments to regulate activities and enforce laws on Indian lands." IGRA fully preserved tribal regulatory authority over Class II gaming without state intervention. However, IGRA gave the states a role in determining the scope and extent of tribal gaming by requiring tribal-state compacts for Class III gaming.

IGRA establishes the jurisdictional framework that governs Indian gaming. IGRA establishes three classes of games with a different regulatory scheme for each.

- Class I gaming is defined as traditional and social Indian gaming for minimal prizes. Regulatory authority over Class I gaming is vested exclusively in tribal governments.

- Class II gaming is defined as the game of chance commonly known as bingo (whether or not electronic, computer, or other technological aids are used in connection therewith) and (if played in the same location) pull-tabs, lotto, punchboards, tip jars, instant bingo and other games similar to bingo. Class II gaming also includes non-banked card games. IGRA specifically excludes slot machines or electronic facsimiles of any game of chance from the definition of Class II games. Tribes retain their authority to conduct, license and regulate Class II gaming as long as the state in which the tribe is located permits such gaming for any purpose, and the tribal government adopts a gaming ordinance approved by the Commission. Tribal governments are responsible for regulating Class II gaming, with Commission oversight.

- Class III is defined as all forms of gaming that are neither Class I nor Class II. Games commonly played in casinos, such as slot machines, blackjack, craps, and roulette, fall in the Class III category. Class III gaming is often referred to as full-scale casino-style gaming. As a compromise among tribal, state and Federal interests, IGRA restricts tribal authority to conduct Class III gaming. Before a tribe may lawfully conduct Class III gaming, the following conditions must be met: (1) the facility must be located in a State that permits such gaming for any purpose by any person, organization or entity; (2) the tribe and the state must have negotiated a compact that has been approved by the Secretary of the Interior, or the Secretary must have approved regulatory procedures; and (3) the tribe must have adopted a tribal gaming ordinance that has been approved by the Chair of the Commission. State and tribal governments are primarily responsible for regulating Class III gaming.

Although Congress clearly intended states to address Class III regulatory issues in tribal-state compacts, IGRA did not make this mandatory, and many states accordingly rely upon continued tribal and Federal oversight by the NIGC to address their regulatory concerns regarding Class III tribal gaming under IGRA. Additionally, IGRA tasks the NIGC with a number of specific regulatory functions, such as: approving tribal ordinances for Class II and Class III gaming; approving management contracts; ensuring tribes and management contractors comply with IGRA and Commission rules and regulations; and implementing regulations. Accordingly, the Commission plays a key role in the oversight and regulation of both Class II and Class III gaming.

Commission Structure

The Commission provides Federal oversight to over 400 tribally owned, operated or licensed gaming establishments operating in 28 states. The Commission maintains its headquarters in Washington, DC, and has seven regional offices and three satellite offices. The Commission is divided into four separate divisions with a combined staff of over 100 full-time employees, as of 2012. Approximately half of the Commission staff is assigned to headquarters in Washington, DC, with the remaining staff assigned to regional offices located in Portland, Oregon; Sacramento, California; Phoenix, Arizona; St. Paul, Minnesota; Tulsa, Oklahoma; Washington, DC; and Oklahoma City, Oklahoma; and satellite offices in Rapid City, South Dakota; Temecula, California; and Flowood, Mississippi.

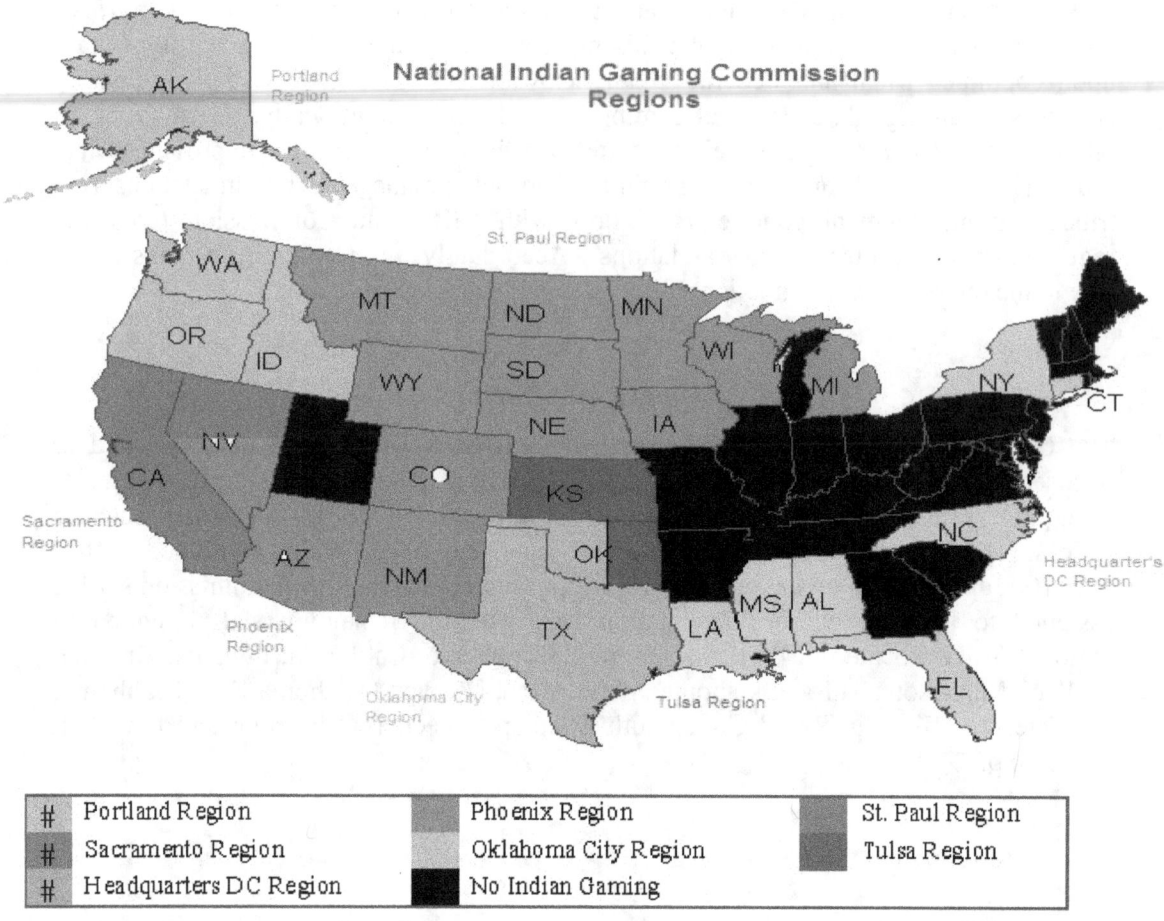

National Indian Gaming Commission Regions

#	Portland Region		Phoenix Region		St. Paul Region
#	Sacramento Region		Oklahoma City Region		Tulsa Region
#	Headquarters DC Region		No Indian Gaming		

The Commission established its field offices to improve the level and quality of services it provides to tribes, and to enhance its ability to communicate, collaborate and interact with tribes located within each office's geographic region. The field offices are vital to carrying out the statutory responsibilities of the Commission. By having auditors and compliance officers close to tribal gaming facilities, the Commission seeks to facilitate compliance with the Act and foster better relationships with tribal leaders, officials and regulatory personnel. In addition to auditing and investigative activities, the field staff provides technical assistance and training to promote a better understanding of gaming controls within the regulated industry, and to enhance cooperation and compliance to ensure the integrity of gaming operations.

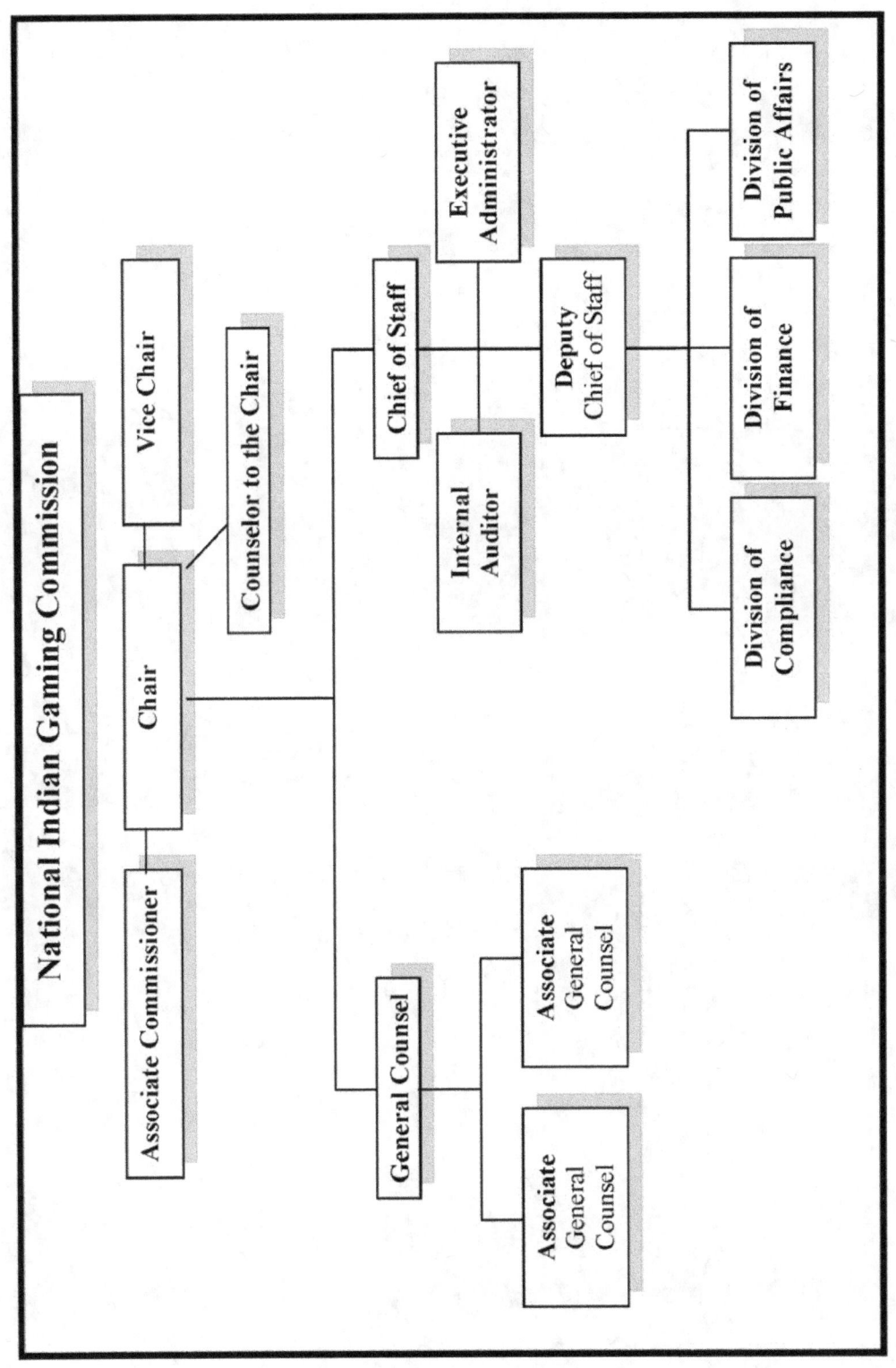

Budget Priorities

Currently, the industry consists of over 400 Indian gaming operations in 28 states. These operations are owned, operated, or licensed by more than 230 tribal governments. The industry generated $27.2 billion of gross gaming revenues in 2011.

As with any industry, technology continues to evolve, resulting in both greater efficiencies and new challenges. In order to keep pace with changes in technology, financial resources must be directed to training Commission staff and to providing training to tribal gaming operators and regulators to assure their ability to regulate and safeguard their operations.

Background

Prior to 1997, the Commission was legislatively prohibited from collecting fees in excess of $1.5 million annually. The 1998 Interior Appropriations Act (P.L. 105-83) expanded the fee base to include Class III (casino style) gaming and raised the limitation on annual fee collections to $8 million. In the 2003, 2004, 2005, and 2006 Interior Appropriations Acts, the Congress enacted a general provision raising this limitation to $12 million for fiscal years 2004, 2005, 2006, and 2007 respectively. On May 12, 2006, the Native American Technical Corrections Act of 2006 was enacted providing a new basis for determining the fee limitation.

The newly enacted legislation provided a fee limitation that allowed the Commission to maintain a fee collection level in proportion to the size of the industry it oversees. With fees now capped at 0.080% of the industry's gross revenue, the Commission's funding will expand or contract in proportion to the growth or contraction of the Indian gaming industry.

Another change included in Public Law 109-221 was the requirement that the Commission, like other Federal agencies, be subject to the Government Performance and Results Act of 1993 (GPRA), and that any plan instituted in compliance with GPRA include technical assistance to tribal gaming operations. To that end, on January 8, 2009, the NIGC submitted its GPRA Strategic Plan for Fiscal Years 2009 to 2014 to Congress and the Office of Management and Budget (OMB).

Annual Fees for Operations

The Commission assesses annual fees on tribal gaming revenues in accordance with procedures set forth in 25 C.F.R. Part 514. In 2012, the Commission promulgated changes to these regulations that became effective on October 1, 2012. Per the new regulation, on or before March 1, the Commission will publish a preliminary fee rate. If necessary, changes to the fee rate will be published no later than June 1 of that year. The rate must be sufficient to generate income to fund the annual operation of the Commission, and to maintain a transition balance for the upcoming year's operation.

Each gaming operation must submit quarterly payments for fees assessed by three, six, nine, and twelve months after the end of their fiscal year.

Maintenance of the transition balance is essential to the fiscal integrity of the Commission because the unique statutory provisions governing the Commission's funding subject it to significant cash flow variations. Unlike other Federal agencies, the Commission's authorizing legislation does not provide for full funding at the beginning of each fiscal year. Instead, the Commission receives quarterly payments equal to approximately 1/4 of each gaming operation's projected annual fee assessment. The carryover transition balance is necessary to cover the first and second quarter of operation until the fees are actually received and credited to the operating account. For example, fees collected on or before the December 31, 2013 due date will provide the operational capital for the first three months of calendar year 2014. The Commission attempts to maintain a transition balance to fund the first two quarters of the new year in order to absorb any cash flow variations that may occur.

Tab:2014 Budget

DEPARTMENT OF THE INTERIOR
NATIONAL INDIAN GAMING COMMISSION

Narrative Summary Statement

The Indian Gaming Regulatory Act (Public Law 100-497) established, within the Department of the Interior, the National Indian Gaming Commission. The Commission monitors and regulates gaming activities conducted on Indian lands. The Commission fosters the economic development of Indian tribes by ensuring the integrity of Indian gaming and ensuring that the tribes are the primary beneficiaries of their gaming revenues. Operating costs of the Commission are financed through annual assessments of gaming operations regulated by the Commission consistent with provisions of the Native American Technical Corrections Act of 2006 (Public Law 109-221).

Summary of the Fiscal Year 2014 Budget

Permanent Appropriation

The Indian Gaming Regulatory Act, as amended, established the National Indian Gaming Commission to monitor and participate in the regulation of gaming conducted on Indian lands. The NIGC's operational costs are financed through annual assessments of gaming operations regulated by the Commission.

All costs associated with the Commission's operation during fiscal year 2014 will be derived from fees assessed on, and collected from, the regulated Indian gaming industry. The Commission will continue its consultation with the affected tribes and evaluate their input prior to implementing the proposed budget. The revenue to be collected in 2014 will assure funding to address the full-year impact of new hires. The Commission will continue to maintain a carryover balance sufficient to assure that cash flow variations do not impact ongoing operations. Fees are paid quarterly, based on each gaming operation's assessable gross revenue. This system often results in cash flow variations, and therefore a transition balance, derived from prior year funds carried forward to the new fiscal year, is essential for continuity of operations.

With an actual employee count of 97 at the end of 2012 to the projected 115 in 2013 and 2014, the NIGC is forecasting full-year obligations of $19 million in fiscal year 2013 and $20 million in fiscal year 2014. This will allow the Commission to hire additional local and field personnel to implement its responsibilities under the Act. These funds will also be used to upgrade and improve the NIGC's information management system, and expand technical assistance and training. This forecast includes expenditures for oversight of class III gaming, as provided by applicable law such as tribal gaming ordinances and tribal-state compacts.

Reimbursable Expenses

The NIGC conducts background investigations of individuals and entities with a financial interest in, or management responsibility for, potential management contracts. Pursuant to the 25 U.S.C § 2711(e), these investigations are conducted to determine whether the contracts can be approved. In accordance with § 2711(i), the Commission is reimbursed from the potential contractors to conduct these background investigations and also for fingerprint processing costs.

Fee Regulation

The regulations implementing the legislative provisions governing the collection of fees allow the Commission to collect the statutory maximum allowed by Congress:

§514.14 Annual Fees

    (a) The total amount of all fees imposed during any fiscal year shall not exceed the statutory maximum imposed by Congress. The Commission shall credit pro-rata any fees collected in excess of this amount against amounts otherwise due according to §514.4.

Additionally, in 2012, NIGC regulations were amended to specifically address the collection of fees for fingerprint processing:

§ 514.15 May tribes submit fingerprint cards to the NIGC for processing?

Tribes may submit fingerprint cards to the Commission for processing by the Federal Bureau of Investigation (FBI) and the Commission may charge a fee to process fingerprint cards on behalf of the tribes.

§ 514.16 How does the Commission adopt the fingerprint processing fee?

(a) The Commission shall review annually the costs involved in processing fingerprint cards and, by a vote of not less than two of its members, shall adopt preliminary rates for each calendar year no later than March 1st of that year, and, if considered necessary, shall modify those rates no later than June 1st of that year.

(b) The fingerprint fee charge shall be based on fees charged by the Federal Bureau of Investigation and costs incurred by the Commission. Commission costs include Commission personnel, supplies, equipment costs, and postage to submit the results to the requesting tribe.

§ 514.17 How are fingerprint processing fees collected by the Commission?

(a) Fees for processing fingerprint cards will be billed monthly to each Tribe for cards processed during the prior month. Tribes shall pay the amount billed within forty-five (45) days of the date of the bill.

(b) The Chair may suspend fingerprint card processing for a tribe that has a bill remaining unpaid for more than forty-five (45) days.

(c) Fingerprint fees shall be sent to the following address: Comptroller, National Indian Gaming Commission, 1441 L Street NW., Suite 9100, Washington, DC 20005. Checks should be made payable to the National Indian Gaming Commission (do not remit cash).

Authorization:

Indian Gaming Regulatory Act, Public Law 100-497, as amended.

Objectives:

To regulate and monitor gaming conducted on Indian lands and to protect Indian gaming as a means of generating tribal revenues.

Program Activities:

The Commission's mission is to effectively monitor and participate in the regulation of Indian gaming pursuant to the Indian Gaming Regulatory Act (IGRA) in order to promote the integrity of the Indian gaming industry. To affect these goals, the Commission is authorized to conduct investigations, undertake enforcement actions including the issuance of notices of violation, assessment of civil fines, issuance of closure orders, approve management contracts, and issue such regulations as necessary to meet its responsibilities under the Act.

The Act grants broad authority to the Commission and provides authority to the Chair to:

- issue temporary closure orders
- levy civil fines, of up to $25,000 per violation per day, against a tribe, management contractor, or individual operator for violation of the Act, the regulations or a tribal gaming ordinance
- approve tribal gaming ordinances
- approve gaming management contracts
- appoint and supervise staff

The Commission as a whole is empowered to:

- monitor gaming activities
- inspect gaming premises
- conduct background investigations
- inspect records relating to gaming
- approve the annual budget
- adopt regulations for the assessment and collection of civil fines
- adopt a schedule of annual fees
- issue permanent closure orders
- adopt regulations as deemed appropriate to implement the provisions of IGRA

Together the Commission serves as an appellate body. Aggrieved parties may appeal decisions of the Chair to the full Commission.

In carrying out these responsibilities, the Commission also:

- provides education, training and technical assistance regarding applicable regulatory requirements
- assists tribes with background investigations and fingerprint processing
- receives and processes appeals
- conducts formal and informal hearings
- consults with Indian tribes, states and the regulated community
- defends against lawsuits challenging the Commission's actions
- issues advice and guidance through bulletins, advisory opinions and other publications
- provides audits and other evaluative services

DEPARTMENT OF THE INTERIOR
NATIONAL INDIAN GAMING COMMISSION
Special Fund Receipt/Expenditure Account
Gaming Activity Fees
(in millions of dollars)

Identification code 14-5141-0-2-806	2012 Actual	2013 Estimate	2014 Estimate
01.99 Balance, start of year................................	-	-	-
Receipts:			
02.00 NIGC, Gaming activity fees........................	19	19	19
02.99 Total receipts and collections....................	19	19	19
04.00 Total: Balances and Collections...............	19	19	19
Appropriations:			
National Indian Gaming Commission			
05.00 NIGC, Gaming activity fees........................	-19	-19	-19
05.99 Total appropriations.................................	-19	-19	-19
07.99 Balance, end of year..............................	-	-	-

Program and Financing (in millions of dollars)

	2012 Actual	2013 Estimate	2014 Estimate
Obligations by program activity:			
00.01 Direct Program Activity	16	19	20
09.00 Total new obligations...............................	16	19	20
Budgetary Resources:			
Unobligated balance:			
10.00 Unobligated balance brought forward, Oct 1..........	5	8	8
Budget Authority			
Appropriations mandatory:			
12.01 Appropriation (special or trust fund):.................	19	19	19
12.60 Appropriations, mandatory (total)...................	19	19	19
19.30 Total budgetary resources available...................	24	27	27
Memorandum (non-add) entries:			
19.41 Unexpired unobligated balance, end of year...........	8	8	7
Change in obligated balance:			
Obligated balance, start of year (net):			
30.00 Unpaid obligations, brought forward, Oct (gross)...	1	1	1
30.10 Obligations incurred, unexpired accounts...............	16	19	20
30.20 Outlays (gross).......................................	-16	-19	-20
Obligated balance, end of year (net):			
30.50 Unpaid obligations, end of year	1	1	1
32.00 Obligated balance, end of year	1	1	1
Budget authority and outlays, net\:			
Mandatory:			
40.90 Budget authority, gross..............................	19	19	19
Outlays, gross:			
41.00 Outlays from new mandatory authority..................	16	18	18
41.01 Outlays from mandatory balances....................	---	1	2
41.10 Outlays, gross (total)...............................	16	19	20
41.60 Budget authority, net (mandatory)...................	19	19	19
41.70 Outlays, net (mandatory)............................	16	19	20
41.80 Budget authority, net (total).......................	19	19	19
41.90 Outlays, net (total)................................	16	19	20

DEPARTMENT OF THE INTERIOR
NATIONAL INDIAN GAMING COMMISSION
Special Fund Receipt/Expenditure Account
Gaming Activity Fees

Object Classification (in millions of dollars)

Identification code 14-5141-0-2-806		2012 Actual	2013 Estimate	2014 Estimate
Direct obligations				
11.11	Personnel compensation: Full-time permanent..	10	11	12
11.21	Civilian personnel benefits.......................	3	3	3
12.10	Travel and transportation of persons......	1	1	1
12.31	Rental payments to GSA...........................	1	1	1
12.52	Other Services..	1	2	2
19.90	Subtotal, direct obligations....................	16	18	19
99.95	Below reporting threshold........................	---	1	1
99.99	Total new obligations..............................	16	19	20

Personnel Summary

	2012 Actual	2013 Estimate	2014 Estimate
Total compensable workyears			
Full-time equivalent employment	100	115	115

DEPARTMENT OF THE INTERIOR
NATIONAL INDIAN GAMING COMMISSION
Reimbursable Activity
(in millions of dollars)

Program and Financing

Identification code 14-0118-0-2-806	2012 Actual	2013 Estimate	2014 Estimate
Obligations by program activity:			
08.01 Reimbursable Program Activity	2	2	2
09.00 Total new obligations...	2	2	2
Budgetary resources:			
Unobligated balance:			
10.00 Unobligated balance brought forward, Oct 1...	2	2	2
Budget authority:			
Spending authority from offsetting collections, discretionary			
17.00 Collected..	2	2	2
17.50 Spending authority from offsetting collections, disc (total).	2	2	2
19.30 Total budgetary resources available.......................	4	4	4
Memorandum (non-add) entries:.................................			
19.41 Unexpired unobligated balance, end of year........................	2	2	2
Change in obligated balance:......................................			
Obligated balance, start of year (net):			
30.00 Unpaid obligations, brought forward, Oct 1 (gross)..............	---	---	---
30.10 Obligations incurred, unexpired accounts............................	2	2	2
30.20 Outlays (gross)...	-2	-2	-2
Obligated balance, end of year (net):			
30.50 Unpaid obligations, end of year	---	---	---
Memorandum (non-add) entries:.................................			
31.00 Obligated balance, start of year:.............................	---	---	---
32.00 Obligated balance, end of year:..............................	---	---	---
Budget authority and outlays, net:			
Discretionary			
40.00 Budget authority, gross..............................	2	2	2
Outlays, gross:			
40.10 Outlays from new discretionary authority............................	2	2	2
40.11 Outlays from discretionary balances...................................	---	---	---
40.20 Outlays, gross (total)...	2	2	2
Offsets against gross budget authority and outlays:			
Offsetting collections (collected) from:...............................			
40.33 Non-federal sources..	-2	-2	-2
40.70 Budget authority, net (discretionary)......................................	---	---	---
40.80 Outlays, net (discretionary)	---	---	---

DEPARTMENT OF THE INTERIOR

NATIONAL INDIAN GAMING COMMISSION
General and Special Funds: Salaries and Expenses

Object Classification (in millions of dollars)

Identification code 14-0118-0-4-806	2012 Actual	2013 Estimate	2014 Estimate
Reimbursable obligations			
22.52 Other services from non-Federal sources............	2	2	2

DEPARTMENT OF THE INTERIOR
NATIONAL INDIAN GAMING COMMISSION
EMPLOYEE COUNT BY GRADE OR GRADE EQUIVALENT

	2012 Actual	2013 Estimate	2014 Estimate
EX-IV	1	1	1
EX-V	2	2	2
ES-4	0	1	1
ES-3	0	0	0
ES-1	0	0	0
GS-15	11	13	13
GS-14	15	17	17
GS-13	30	37	37
GS-12	20	22	22
GS-11	2	5	5
GS-10	2	3	3
GS-09	4	4	4
GS-08	0	0	0
GS-07	0	0	0
GS-06	10	10	10
GS-05	0	0	0
Total FTE	**97**	**115**	**115**

In accordance with the Act, appointments are made without regard to the provisions of Title 5, U.S. Code governing appointments in the competitive services

Tab:Graphs

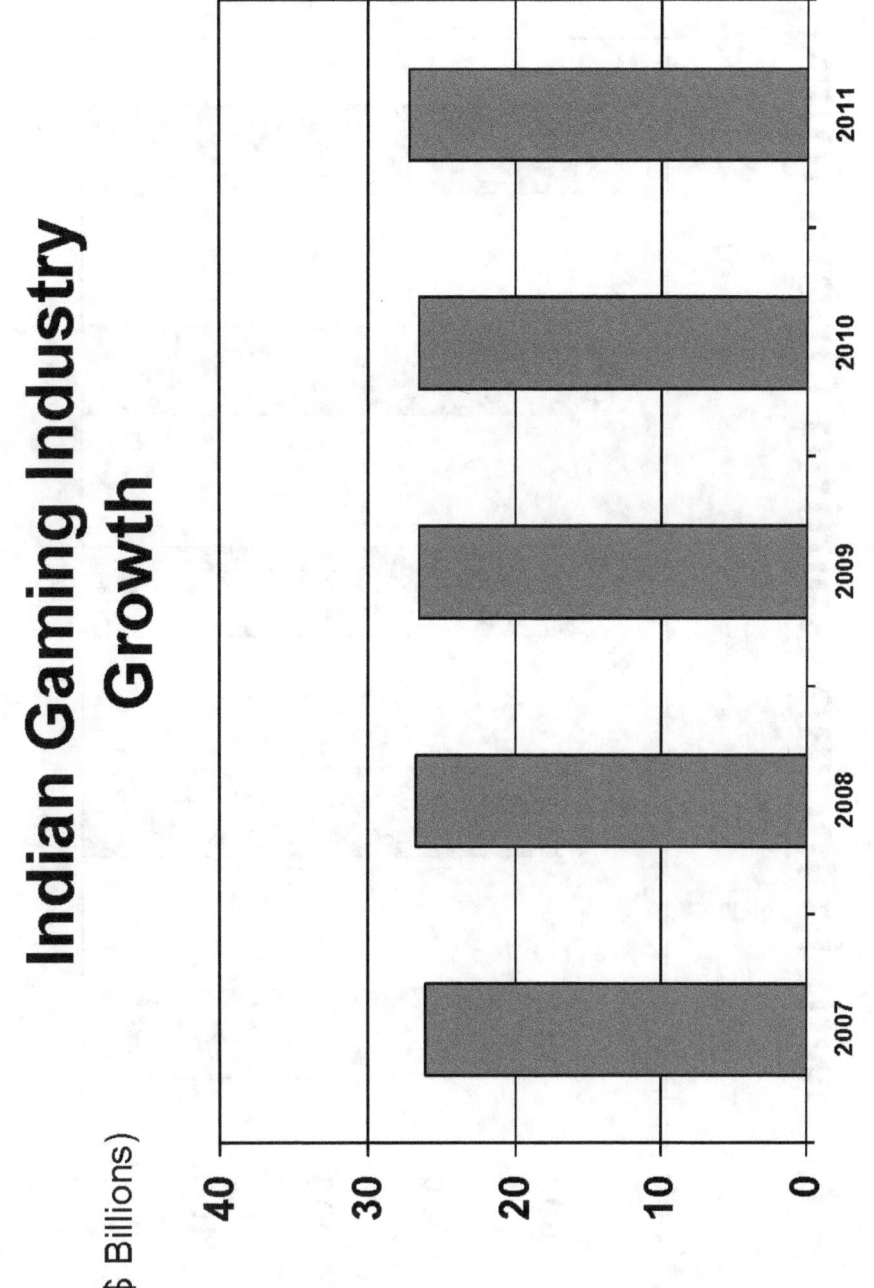

Indian Gaming Industry Growth

($ Billions)

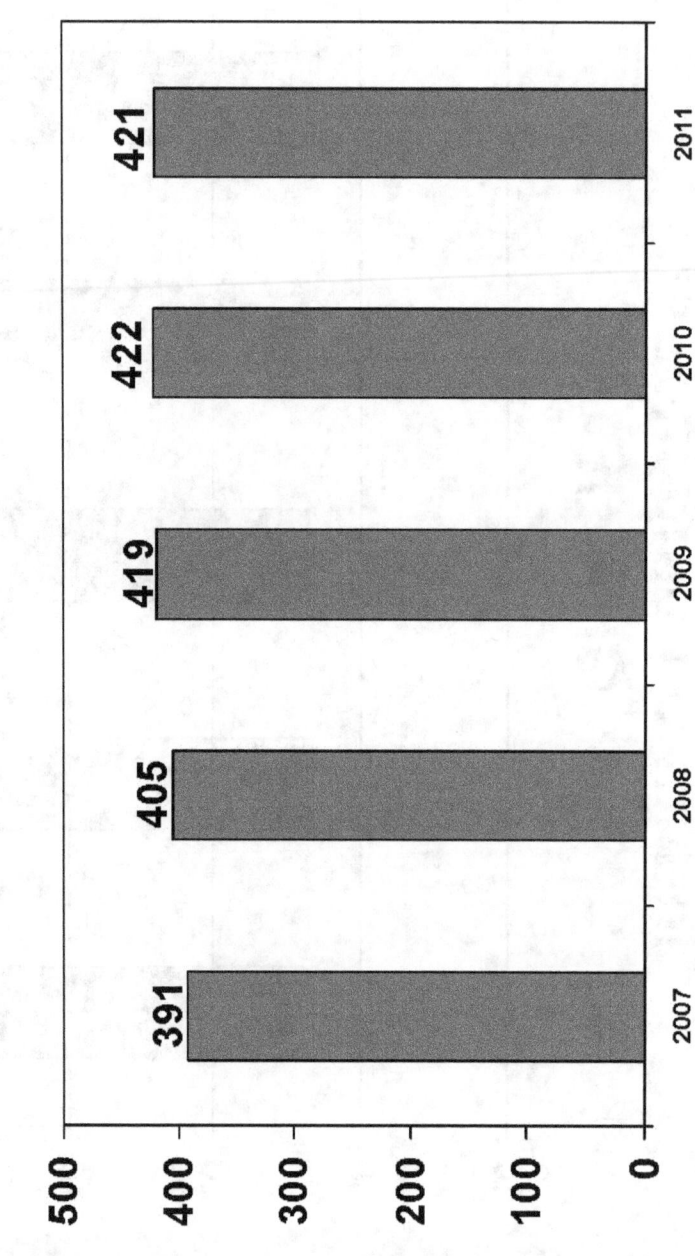

Growth in Indian Gaming Operations

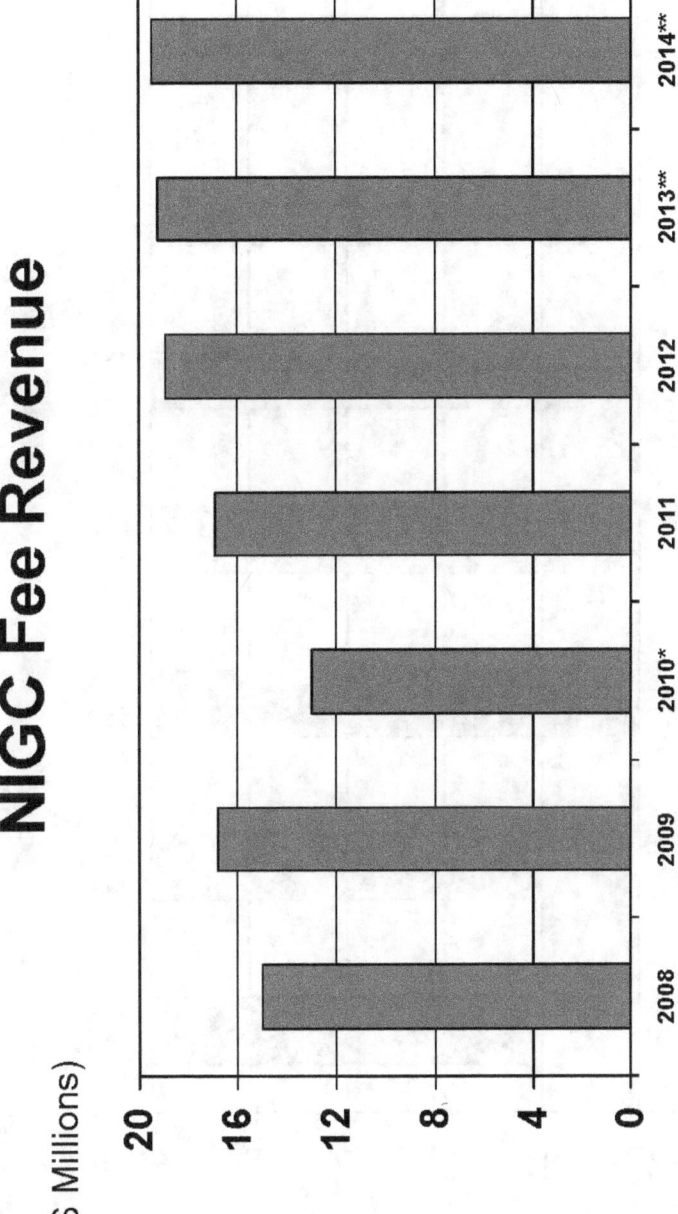

NIGC Fee Revenue

($ Millions)

* Fiscal Year 2010 included only ¾ of a year's payments

** Forecast

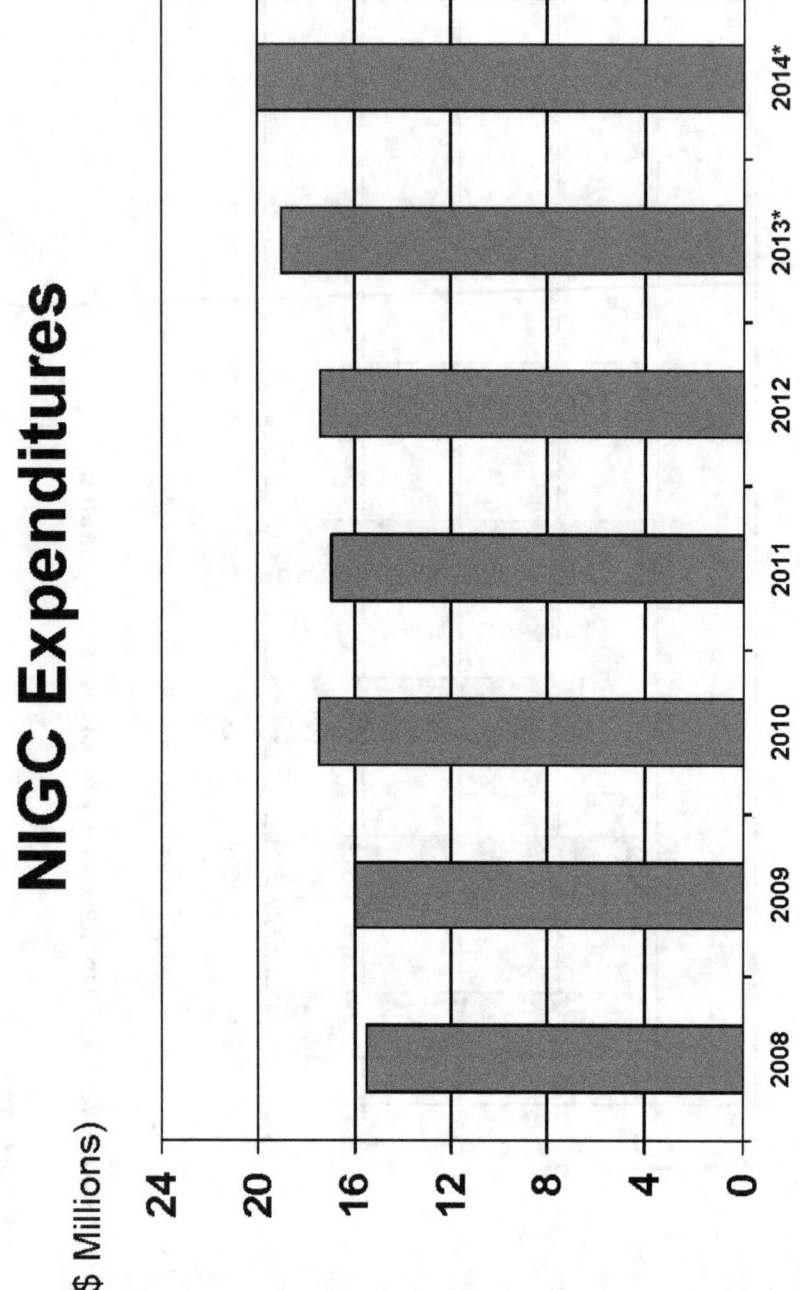

NIGC Expenditures

($ Millions)

2008 | 2009 | 2010 | 2011 | 2012 | 2013* | 2014*

* Forecast

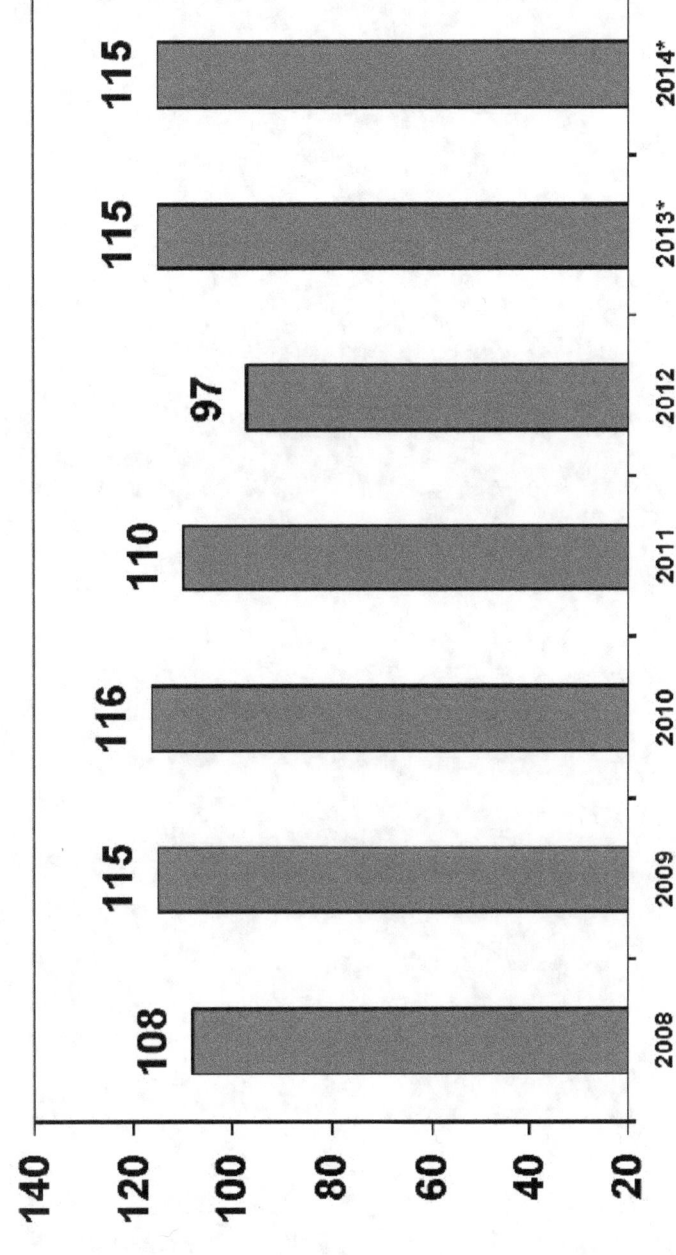

Staffing Levels

* Forecast

Tab:GPRA Information

Government Performance and Results Act Information

In 2006, Congress amended the Indian Gaming Regulatory Act, 25 U.S.C. §§ 2701 – 2721, Pub. L. 100-497, and for the first time made the National Indian Gaming Commission subject to the Government Performance and Results Act of 1993 (GPRA), Pub. L. 103-62. That obligation is set out at 25 U.S.C. § 2706(d)(1), which states: "In carrying out any action under this chapter, the Commission shall be subject to the Government Performance and Results Act off 1993."

On September 30, 2007, the Commission filed its first GPRA performance and accountability report with the Office of Management and Budget (OMB). One year later, on September 18, 2008, the Commission released a draft five-year strategic plan for review and comment, and it published the final five-year strategic plan on January 8, 2009.

GRPA requires that an agency's "strategic plan shall be updated and revised at least every three years." 5 U.S.C. § 306(b). Consistent with this obligation and the Commission's vision of adhering to principles of good government including transparency to promote agency accountability and fiscal responsibility, the Commission has completed four Tribal Consultation sessions for comment and review of a new Strategic Plan for years 2014-2018.

Summary and Highlights of Commission Activities

During FY 2012, the Commission's four primary initiatives consisted of consulting and building relationships with tribal governments, providing technical assistance and training, continuing its regulatory review, and reviewing its internal operations. As such, during the past fiscal year, the Commission accomplished the following goals and tasks.

- The Commission continued its Assistance, Compliance, and Enforcement ("ACE") initiative, which emphasizes working with tribal, states, and Federal regulators to ensure effective coordination in the regulation of Indian gaming, working with tribes to ensure compliance with IGRA, and when necessary, taking enforcement action for violations of IGRA.

- The Commission conducted 17 tribal consultations as part of its regulatory review.

- The Commission has published 25 C.F.R. Subchapter H; Part 559; Part 502; Part 573; Part 571; and Part 537. The Commission has repealed obsolete regulation 25 C.F.R. Part 523.

- In response to the need to develop a comprehensive set of regulation specific to Class II Gaming, the agency allocated personnel to work with an advisory committee composed of tribal representatives to create 25 C.F.R. Part 543 and Part 547. Both regulations have become final rules.

- Effective October 1, 2012 NIGC re-implemented the submission of fees and worksheets on a quarterly basis, pursuant to the regulatory changes to 25 C.F.R. §514. Training and technical assistance is being offered to gaming tribes regarding the changes to this regulation.

- During FY 2011, the Agency began the process of conducting a reorganization of the Commission to better utilize existing resources and promote efficiency. The Commission continues to implement its reorganization to ensure effective approaches to carry out its obligations under IGRA.

- Completed a GSA Request for Proposal for office space to prepare for NIGC Headquarters relocation.

- The NIGC increased the amount of training offered to gaming tribes throughout the United States. The topics of the courses offered were in direct response to tribal requests for specific training. During FY 2012, the NIGC conducted approximately 84 training events comprising approximately 748.3 training hours, and attended by approximately 2,013 training participants.

- The Commission continued the process of better targeting its training activities and agency resources by identifying partnerships, improving training offerings, and utilizing technology to more effectively reach target audiences.

- During FY 2010, the NIGC established and implemented a program to perform abbreviated audits to approximately 13 California tribes conducting Class III gaming to assess compliance with NIGC Minimum Internal Control Standards (MICS).

During FY 2012, the NIGC conducted 13 abbreviated Class III MICS audits and 1 comprehensive MICS audit.

- Commission auditors also performed 3 comprehensive MICS audits and 4 cursory MICS audits specific to class II gaming operations. The audit findings were included in reports delivered to the audited tribes. The Commission will offer technical assistance to the tribes in identifying and implementing remedial action.

- The NIGC Chair approved: one management contract; six amendment(s) to an approved management contract; and three modifications to the List of Individuals and Entities with a direct or indirect financial interest in, or management responsibility for contracts with nine Tribes involving 30 individuals. The Commission also conducted financial background investigations on certain persons and entities associated with the management contractors.

- The Commission processed approximately 67,421 fingerprint cards for tribal gaming commissions.

- The Commission began the update of its strategic plan to cover FY 2014 – 2018. Four consultation meetings were conducted to review the plan and for the public to provide comments on the plan.

- Began the electronic conversion of documents, forms and manuals to improve operational efficiency.

- The Commission drafted (or revised) and adopted internal agency policies related to the following subjects: (i) performance appraisal system; (ii) transportation subsidies; (iii) special pay entitlements; (iv) awards and employee recognition program; and (v) travel policy. A review of position descriptions was conducted and will continue to be better aligned with job duties.

- The Commission completed a draft consultation policy that will be posted for tribal comment.

- Continued to maintain and update the Commission's data systems in tracking each of the tribal gaming facilities to enhance communication.

- Completed an IT assessment of need and will continue to research options for best utilization of financial resources.

Continuing with its four primary initiatives, during FY 2013, the Commission is working on the following goals and tasks:

- The Commission continues to implement ACE to facilitate compliance throughout all regions, and continues to build upon relationships with tribal, Federal, and state regulatory and/or law enforcement agencies.

- The Commission continues to review and update its regulations to maintain the integrity of Indian gaming. The Commission will continue to consult with tribes as part of its regulatory review.

- During FY 2011, the Agency began the process of conducting a reorganization of the Commission to better utilize existing resources and promote efficiency. The Commission continues to implement its reorganization to ensure effective approaches to carry out its obligations under IGRA.

- Continue planning for upcoming NIGC headquarters office move that includes working with GSA on space allocation and lease options.

- The Commission continues to work on drafting (or revising) and adopting additional internal agency policies related to the following subjects: (i) procedures for providing reasonable accommodation for individuals with disabilities; (ii) standards of ethical conduct; (iii) telework program; (iv) training and employee development; (v) promotion; (vi) time, attendance, and leave policies; (vii) government charge card programs; and (viii) nursing mothers program.

- The Commission continues to respond to requests from tribes for technical assistance, and increase both the amount and breadth of technical assistance provided. It utilizes all forms of training forums and locations to better reach targeted audiences being mindful of Commission and tribal financial resources. The Commission continues to provide training to tribes within all seven NIGC regions. The Commission continues to update the training catalog as necessary.

- The Commission is coordinating efforts to modernize the NIGC IT network to improve and maintain reliability and manageability.

- The Commission will finalize its strategic plan covering FY 2014 – 2018.

- The Commission will improve it records management system, including paper and electronic records.

- During FY 2013, the Commission continues to work on its everyday tasks, including:
    - performing MICS audits specific to Class II gaming operations.

    - responding to requests from tribal gaming operators and regulators for IGRA and gaming related training and technical assistance.

    - working with tribes on the Tribal Access Portal (TAP), a database that enables tribal gaming regulators who are engaged in issuing gaming licenses to check whether a license applicant has a licensing history with any other gaming tribe. Along with information provided by the NIGC/FBI fingerprint submission service, the TAP system assists tribes to complete their own comprehensive background investigation of prospective license applicants.

    - updating its database with accumulated financial data from the gaming operations' audited financial statements and AUP report filings. The Commission establishes a preliminary and final rate utilizing this data.

    - performing internal audits of NIGC departments to increase the Commission's efficiency, effectiveness, and compliance with Federal regulations.

    - reviewing management contracts and amendments to management contracts.

- Processing fingerprint cards for tribal gaming employees as they are submitted by the tribal gaming commissions and tracking payment for fingerprint processing.

- Continuing to respond to technical assistance requests from tribes.

As part of its program objectives for fiscal year 2014, the Commission plans to:

- Continue support of the NIGC High Priority Performance Goals as identified in the Strategic Plan.

- Continue efforts to modernize the NIGC IT network to improve and maintain reliability and manageability.

- Implement updated strategic plan.

- Continue its regulatory review which it began during FY 2011 and implement its new and/or revised regulations, and to provide training to tribes on compliance with any new requirements.

- Continue the development of the Commission's internal administrative and personnel manual, and develop and implement corresponding training programs.

- Continue to inform the public about the Commission's activities through various media and training resources.

- Coordinate and provide training events to tribal entities in each of the seven regions.

- Continue to respond to requests from tribes for technical assistance, and increase both the amount and breadth of technical assistance provided. Utilize all forms of training forums and locations to better reach targeted audiences being mindful of Commission and tribal financial resources. The Commission continues to update the training catalog as necessary.

- Continue to perform MICS and other types of compliance audits to maintain the integrity of gaming industry.

- Continue to implement the requirements of GPRA, including the development and implementation of a performance measurement system.

- Maintain a consistently high level of compliance for the submission of gaming activity fees and external year-end audits through continued monitoring and contact with gaming tribes, with an emphasis on voluntary compliance.

- Improve operational efficiency through enhanced records management that includes the electronic conversion of documents, forms and manuals.

- Establish a training and employee development program in order to attract and retain highly-qualified personnel. The agency will annually assess the skills of its employees and provide necessary training.

www.ingramcontent.com/pod-product-compliance
Lightning Source LLC
Chambersburg PA
CBHW080921290526
45795CB00007BA/2607